WORLD MYTHS AND LEGENDS II

The Caribbean

Flora Foss

Upper Saddle River,
New Jersey

World Myths and Legends
Greek and Roman
Ancient Middle Eastern
Norse
African
Far Eastern
Celtic
Native American
Regional American

World Myths and Legends II
India
Russia
Europe
South America
The Caribbean
Central America
Mexico
Southeast Asia

Series Editor: Joseph T. Curran
Cover Designer: Dianne Platner
Text Designer: Teresa A. Holden
Interior Illustrations: Mary Beth Gaitskill
Cover Photo: The Granger Collection, New York

Copyright © 1993 by Globe Fearon, Inc., One Lake Street, Upper Saddle River, New Jersey, 07458, www.globefearon.com. All rights reserved. No part of this book may be reproduced by any means, transmitted, or translated into a machine language without the written permission of the publisher.

Library of Congress Catalog Card Number: 92-72301
ISBN 0-8224-4632-4
Printed in the United States of America.

5 6 7 8 9 10 04 03 02 01 00
EB

CONTENTS

*An Introduction to the Myths
and Legends of the Caribbean*   v

1   In the Beginning

The Fish in the Gourd
(Ancient Taino)   1
The First People on Earth
(Ancient Carib)   5

2   Gods and People

Father of the Forest *(Trinidad)*   14
The Island of Peace *(Haiti)*   27
The Pointing Tree *(Puerto Rico)*   32

3   Good and Evil

The Fireball Woman *(Trinidad)*   37
Greedy Mariana *(Haiti)*   43
The Magic Orange Tree *(Haiti)*   49
The Wedding Guests *(Puerto Rico)*   57

4 Wisdom and Foolishness

Bringing Back the Dead *(Haiti)*	64
Turtle's Trip *(Haiti)*	68
The Parrot Who Wouldn't Say "Cataño" *(Puerto Rico)*	72
The Doctor Outwits Death *(Dominican Republic)*	80

5 Tricksters

Anansi's Riding Horse *(Jamaica)*	85
Bouki's Dance *(Haiti)*	93
The Servant *(Cuba)*	102
Why Rabbit Has Long Ears *(Cuba)*	110
Pronunciation Guide	117

An Introduction to the Myths and Legends of the Caribbean

In the warm waters of the Caribbean Sea there are many islands. Cuba, Jamaica, Puerto Rico, Haiti, and the Dominican Republic are the largest ones. There are also many small islands, from the Bahamas near Florida to Trinidad and Tobago near Venezuela. All these islands together are sometimes called the Antilles.

Many centuries ago, Arawak and Carib Indians lived on the coast of South America. They could see mountains rising in the distance. Some of the Indians hollowed out trees to make canoes and traveled to the nearest Caribbean islands to live.

Over the years, their numbers grew. The Indians migrated to more and more islands, until their villages dotted all the Antilles.

Arawakan tribes, such as the Taino, were peaceful and lived in fear of the warlike Caribs. Little else brought any fear to the Indians in this beautiful land where it was always warm.

Like people of all cultures, they made stories to explain their world. These ancient stories speak to the deepest feelings people have about the mystery of life.

Each generation told their stories to the next. They passed on their beliefs of how the world began. They told how people came to live on earth and how food was created. For centuries, little changed in their culture.

Then, in 1492, ships from Europe set sail under the trade winds. Columbus and his Spanish crew landed on one of the Caribbean islands. For the first time, the natives saw fair-skinned people with metal weapons and armor. Starting then, many changes began.

The European explorers were looking for gold and rich trade with India. They found instead islands with rich soil and a prized location. Here they could raise valuable crops and establish military seaports. The Spanish became the first colonists. Later, French and British soldiers would also vie for some of the rich Caribbean land.

This conquest meant death for the natives. The Spanish took their lands and tried to make slaves of the Arawaks and Caribs. The Indians had no weapons made of iron. The peace-loving Arawaks were no match for the soldiers. Those that were not killed in battle died in slavery or of European diseases. The Caribs were more fierce, but they, too, were defeated. Today, only a few hundred Caribs of pure native blood remain.

The colonists wanted slave labor to carve out vast sugar plantations. This crop could bring great wealth. With the Indians gone, though, the colonists lost their laborers. Therefore, the trade winds were used again to bring ships to the Antilles, carrying a shameful cargo.

Hundreds of ships brought men, women, and children from West Africa. For over three hundred years, millions of African people were forced to the islands. Today, they still make up the largest part of the population of the Antilles. The Africans became the slaves who built a rich trade empire. It was only the descendants of the European settlers, however, who became wealthy.

The Africans did hold on to a wealth of myths and legends they brought to the Caribbean. Some of these tales feature talking animals and lovable rascals. Trickster characters are very popular in the Antilles. A trickster uses his wits to defeat a larger, stronger character. Jamaicans tell of the trickster Anansi, who is both spider and man. Haitian people have stories about the trickster Ti Malice.

African religions such as Voodoo also found their way into the stories told in the Caribbean. These stories bring to life many good and evil spirits.

African culture had the strongest influence in the Caribbean, but stories of Europe took root, too. Some tales tell of magic powers, of fairies, and of wicked stepmothers.

The myths and legends of the Caribbean came from many places. They have been spun together over time into a complex web of history, spiritual belief, and human nature. They are alive in a people who share the blood of Africans, Europeans, and Native Americans.

Caribbean myths and legends show the pride of strong people living in harmony with nature. Some of them express the longing for peace and freedom. Still others laugh at human failings or show admiration for the strong, the clever, and the good. In other words, they express the emotions and concerns of people the world over.

The Fish in the Gourd

The Indians of the Caribbean grew crops, but they also relied on fish for food. This myth was told by the Taino Indians, an early group of people who lived in the Caribbean. It explains how the spirits provided fish for the world.

In the beginning, there was Yaya, the Spirit of Spirits. No other spirit was higher or greater than Yaya. There was no power above his. Yaya owned many lands.

His son was called Yayael, which means "Son of Yaya." Yayael grew jealous of his father's power. He finally became so jealous that he plotted to kill his father.

When Yaya found out that Yayael wanted to kill him, he sent his son away. "Go," he commanded. "You are banished from my lands forever."

For a long time, after that, Yayael wandered in faraway places. He did not find good land or sweet water, and he was not happy so far from home. So he returned to his homelands, in spite of his father's command. Yayael had done what was forbidden. Yaya declared that Yayael must pay for his disobedience. With a heavy heart, Yaya killed his son.

Yaya and his wife grieved for Yayael. They put their son's bones in a gourd and hung it from the roof of the house. This way some part of Yayael would always be nearby.

A long time passed. At last Yaya said to his wife, "I wish to be with the spirit of my son. Let us take down the gourd."

Yaya wanted the gourd to use in his spirit dance. He hoped to call up Yayael's spirit by shaking the gourd.

However, Yaya's wife believed magic would return their son to them in his old form. She thought that if she emptied the gourd, perhaps Yayael would appear whole again. Happily, she took down the gourd and turned it over. She eagerly spilled out everything in the gourd.

To their surprise, out of the gourd spilled water and many, many fish! Yayael's bones had turned into large and small fish of every kind.

At first, Yaya and his wife were sad. Not only was there no Yayael, neither could they use the gourd to commune with their son's spirit. The woman and man talked and came to a decision. Yaya declared their decision.

Yaya's wife taking down the gourd

Yaya said, "The water shall become oceans and rivers where fish will live. The fish will multiply to be a wealth of food for the people. Whenever people take the fish and eat them, they will give thanks to the spirits. The fish will become sacred food."

Yaya made the water form the oceans and rivers. Then he made the fish swim in these waters.

This is how the sacred food of the Taino came into the world. The bones of Yayael, son of the Spirit of Spirits, became fish.

1. Why did Yaya banish Yayael?
2. What did Yaya do with his slain son's bones?
3. What happened to Yayael's bones?

The First People on Earth

This ancient Carib myth tells how the first people came to live on the earth. It also explains how they first got food.

People from the Moon

In the beginning, there were no other people but the Caribs. They lived on the moon. They praised the Ancient One, Kabo Tano, for the light and darkness and for all things.

From the moon, the Caribs could see that many worlds moved around them in space. Most of these worlds were bright and shining just as their moon was. However, the Caribs saw one world that was dull and dark. This was the earth. A thick haze hung over it. Year after year, it grew duller and duller. Finally, even the earth's mountaintops were covered with haze.

The Caribs were concerned. The oldest person said, "That earth is a disgrace—so ugly and gray!"

The youngest girl said, "Why don't we polish it?"

"She's right," agreed the strongest Carib. "For generations, we have done nothing while the earth grew duller and duller. We are strong. Let's show that we can make the earth shine the way our moon does."

So the Caribs gathered food and tools and rode to the earth on their cloud chariots. The nearer they got, the worse things looked.

"This will be a difficult job," they thought.

They divided the labor to make it go faster. The young ones scrubbed the gray plains until the grass shone green and the streams sparkled blue. The women scoured the gloom out of the valleys, which allowed radiant flowers and leaves to show. The men polished the dark mountain slopes and tops until they glowed.

Their work was done, and the Caribs were ready to leave the shining earth. They had finished just in time, too, for their food was gone.

The Caribs had worked so hard, they had not noticed when their chariots had quietly drifted away.

"What can we do?" they asked one another fearfully. "Without food, we will starve."

The oldest Carib said, "We must pray to

The Caribs cleaning the earth

Kabo Tano. He will hear us. He will hear our prayers and help us."

All day and night, their cries arose as they called out to Kabo Tano for help. Then they were silent and listened. There was only a deep silence. There was no reply. They were alone.

The Caribs wandered over hot plains and through steamy forests, always looking for food. Some died from hunger. The people were so desperate that they baked big cakes of red clay. They hoped that Kabo Tano would turn the clay to food, but he did not.

In deep distress, they cried out, "Ah, why did we ever leave our home on the moon! We shall all die here without food."

A Tree from Kabo Tano

This time, Kabo Tano answered them. He took pity on the Caribs in their misery and made a great tree. Just one branch was as big as most other whole trees. Every branch bore a different kind of fruit. One held sweet, golden oranges. From another hung bunches of bananas. There were branches full of red and yellow mangoes and others with brown, juicy sapodillas.

In the shade under the tree, Kabo Tano

made many food plants grow. There was cassava, whose roots are so good to eat. There was maize, whose tender ears of corn are so delicious. The flavorful yam grew beneath the soil. Every kind of food plant began to grow.

However, the tree was hidden away, deep in the forest. None of the people had seen it.

One day, Wild Pig found it as he rooted among the leaves. He ate some fallen fruit and some roots and found them all delicious. The marvelous tree became his secret.

Wild Pig soon became round and sleek. He wandered into the village now and then, and the Caribs noticed that he was changing. "How is it," they wondered, "that he grows fat while we waste away like shadows?"

They decided to follow Wild Pig. When he heard their footsteps, he hid himself instead of going to the tree. The Caribs could not find him to follow. They realized they would need help to discover what Wild Pig was eating.

"We can ask Woodpecker for help," the oldest Carib suggested. "He could watch from the treetops and mark the path for us."

They explained to Woodpecker how Wild Pig was growing fat from eating hidden food. Woodpecker was a kindhearted bird and agreed to help them find where Wild Pig ate. In return, the Caribs promised Woodpecker a share of food.

Now Woodpecker was kind and helpful but not very smart. He set out after Wild Pig the next morning. Every now and then, he would stop and tap the tree trunks. Rat-a-tat-tat! Pretty soon Wild Pig noticed the tapping noise behind him.

"Woodpecker is following me," he thought. So he hid himself until Woodpecker gave up and flew off.

Next, the Caribs asked Rat, who was a quiet, skillful hunter. Rat could hide himself so well, surely Wild Pig would be unable to detect him.

The next morning, Wild Pig started out for the great tree. He listened carefully for Woodpecker's tapping. When he heard none, he was satisfied that no one was following him. Wild Pig went straight to the tree of food. He never saw Rat moving silently after him. Soon, Rat knew Wild Pig's secret.

Such a secret it was! Rat tasted the juicy mangoes, the flavorful yams, and the sweet bananas. How tasty and satisfying this good food was!

"This is too great a treasure to share,"

Rat thought. "There are so many Caribs that there would not be enough if they all took some of it."

When Rat returned, he told the Caribs, "Wild Pig was too clever for me. He led me off the track and lost me in the forest."

The disappointed Caribs had to accept Rat's word. They asked him to try again the next day. The next day, Rat's story was much the same. Wild Pig had lost him, he claimed, by swimming across a river.

This went on for a week. Every morning Rat followed Wild Pig and feasted. Every evening he returned with a story of how Wild Pig had eluded him.

By this time, Rat, too, had grown more sleek and rounded. Suspicion grew. Then a keen-eyed Carib noticed bits of food on Rat's whiskers. Despite his cleverness, Rat had to confess.

The Caribs could no longer trust Rat. They held him fast and made him take them to the tree. When they saw it, they stared in wonder. They gazed at the branches, hanging heavy with fruit. They saw the many crops growing in the shadow of the tree. Here at last was plenty.

Food for Everyone

The Caribs began to sing a joyous song of thanks: "All praise the Ancient One, Kabo Tano, for he has given us this precious tree."

Then Kabo Tano spoke to them from a great distance. He commanded, "Cut down the tree."

The Caribs were surprised and afraid. They feared losing the wonderful tree, but they obeyed. They knew the Ancient One must have a good reason for this command. They trusted that he would provide for them.

The men chopped at the mighty trunk with their stone axes. It took many months before the great tree gave way. At last it came crashing to the ground.

The Ancient One spoke again, "You have done well to obey me, my children. Now each of you should take a little of the tree for yourself. You can plant the pieces and grow your own food."

So each of the Caribs took pieces of the branches, trunk, and roots of the tree. They grew their own food trees and plants close to their dwellings. The Caribs then had plenty of food without having to go to the forest.

These plants still provide food. The Caribs found that the earth was a good home.

1. *Why couldn't the Caribs return to their home on the moon?*
2. *What did Kabo Tano create to help the Caribs?*
3. *Why did Kabo Tano command the Caribs to chop down the tree?*

Father of the Forest

In Trinidad, the people tell many stories about spirits. The most popular of all the spirits is Papa Bois, the Father of the Forest. His form is half deer and half man. This story tells how Papa Bois was born and became the protector of the trees and animals.

Long ago there lived a great hunter. He was tall, strong, and very handsome. When he brought his catch home to the city, every eye turned toward him. Men fought for the right to buy from him. Women loved him wildly.

However, he soon grew sick and tired in the hot, crowded city. He felt restless and unhappy.

One morning, the hunter rose early and set out for the farthest forest. His mood lifted as he came closer to the forest. He imagined its coolness with delight.

When he reached the forest's edge, he stopped at a stream. He washed away the dirt and dust of the city until his dark skin shone clean again. He left his clothes beside the stream, picked up his bow and arrows, and entered the deep forest.

The hunter wandered along the animal trails. He felt that the forest was very mysterious and quite beautiful. He heard no animal noises, but he knew animals were there. He felt eyes watching him.

The trail led the man to a stream. When he stooped to drink from it, he heard a noise. A beautiful deer was also drinking at the stream. They saw each other at the same moment. The man stared in amazement. The deer reared back in fright, then fell into the water. She panicked and began to sink.

From the forest, a parrot cried out the deer's name, "Gionda! Gionda!"

Quickly, the hunter dived in and rescued the deer.

The parrot cried, "Our protector is saved! Gionda, Mother of the Forest, is saved!"

The sounds of thankful animals came from throughout the forest. However, the frightened deer struggled free from the hunter's arms and sprang away.

The hunter ran after the deer, but she raced away and disappeared. He searched long and hard, but he could not find the deer. Finally, he was too tired and discouraged to go on. He hung his bow and arrows from a branch. Then he gathered leaves for a bed and went to sleep beneath a huge tree.

Although the hunter did not know it, spirits watched him from the big tree. It was an immortal tree, where gods sometimes lived. It was the oldest and most holy tree in the forest.

These watchers were gods who had led the hunter into the forest to Gionda, the deer. They planned for the hunter and the deer to become mates. It was time for a new kind of spirit to be born, one that was both god and human.

While the hunter slept, Gionda and the animals gathered around him. Sensing that he was being watched, he awoke to see many eyes on him. Then he felt a soft muzzle touch his face. It was Gionda.

"Don't be afraid," she said. "It's only me—Gionda. Don't worry. No one will harm you here in the forest."

"You speak!" the hunter cried. "Why did you run away before?"

She told him of her fear. She talked of how all the forest creatures feared people.

Gionda then told him other things. She explained that she had great powers and watched over the animals and plants. The

Gionda and the hunter

hunter learned that, unlike all the other animals, Gionda was immortal. He also learned that, although she was loved by all the animals, she was lonely.

The hunter looked into her beautiful, gentle eyes and fell in love. Gionda felt a bond with this smooth-skinned creature. She felt that she and the hunter were meant to be together. She saw his shivering, and she warmed him with her body. Then they slept.

A Short Time of Happiness

Dawn came, and the hunter and the deer awoke to see the animals watching them. Gionda introduced the hunter to each animal.

Then a spirit spoke from the immortal tree. "Gionda and Hunter, now you will be married here beneath these holy branches."

Happily the couple stood side by side beneath the tree. There the spirit married them. All the animals trilled and chirped their joy.

Only the snake was unhappy. It was jealous, for it wanted all Gionda's attention. The couple was not aware, though, of this discontent.

The two left the animals and walked

alone. Then Gionda led her husband up a mountain path until they reached the mountaintop. They looked over the whole forest.

She said, "For as long as I can remember, I have ruled this land. It is mine. Now it is yours too. Can you be happy here?"

"It is a world apart, beautiful and peaceful," he replied. "Do you see that far valley?"

Gionda nodded.

"That is the world of humans," he said. "I knew humans once. They are foolish and cannot see what will give them peace. My eyes are clear now. I am sad for the people, but I am glad to have found peace. I will be very happy here with you."

Gionda's heart leapt for joy. That night, they slept peacefully again. However, in the morning, when the hunter awoke, Gionda was gone.

The man wandered the forest, looking for her and calling to the animals for help. The forest was eery and silent and felt cold to the hunter.

A spell had fallen on the forest. The gods, who had led him here, knew he could not remain. This was not the place for a man, even Gionda's mate. One day they would let him return, but for now he must live with people.

Soon the hunter was hopelessly lost. As he wandered in the forest, the snake appeared before him.

"Please," he begged, "help me find Gionda!"

The snake hissed, "You are a hunter. You are an enemy of the forest. You aren't wanted here with us."

With that, it wriggled away. The hunter stumbled on in despair. At last, he came to the edge of the forest where he found his pile of clothes. Sadly, the hunter put them on and returned to the world of people.

Son of the Forest

That morning Gionda had left her sleeping husband to see to the building of their new home. The ancient turtle, the wise one sent by the gods from the spirit world, came to her there.

He said, "Gionda, I have news. An ancient dream will be fulfilled. You will have a child. He will be Son of the Forest. Because of this event, you and your mate will be both mortal and immortal. Like the seasons, your life will blossom and fade and blossom again. You will always love and always live."

Gionda was filled with joy. The turtle continued, "This cannot happen here, though. You must go to Venezuela. You will leave Son of the Forest to take your place. When the fruit of the holy tree turns to gold, I will come to take you to Venezuela. Be ready then for your journey."

Gionda sped through the forest calling joyfully, "A child! A child!" She searched for her mate. Every animal helped her search, except the snake. They could not find the hunter.

Gionda heard the snake laughing and asked, "Have you seen my mate?"

"Yes," the snake lied. "I saw him running from the forest. I called after him and begged him to return. He would not come back."

Gionda could not be comforted. She wept loudly. Then she sadly went to the mountaintop. There she waited, hoping that her mate would return.

There, after some time, the child was born. The animals went to Gionda when they heard of the birth. They marveled at the beautiful baby, Son of the Forest. He was dark-skinned and smooth to the waist like his father. He had strong, furred legs and hooves like his mother.

Gionda felt at peace, but by now the fruit of the holy tree was grown and green. Gionda knew she must prepare to leave.

Son of the Forest must learn all that Gionda knew if he were to take her place. She introduced him to every animal. She taught him the name of every plant and its use, such as for healing or for food. Gionda took her son over every inch of the great forest, making him learn it thoroughly.

Finally, she took him to the mountaintop. There she told him about the world of people. As she told Son of the Forest about his father, she remembered their happiness. Then she looked down at the holy tree and saw that its fruit had turned to gold.

A voice behind Gionda said, "I am back. Are you ready?"

Gionda turned to see that the ancient turtle had returned, as he had promised he would. He waited for her response.

"Yes," she said. "I am nearly ready. I have a few last things to do."

Gionda then gave her blessing to each creature. Then she turned to Son of the Forest. She saw he was grown magically to the size of his father. He was ready to rule the forest.

She said to him, "Love everything that the gods send you. Be strong. These things will make you happy."

Then Gionda climbed onto the ancient turtle's back. They went to the sea, dived in, and Gionda's journey to Venezuela began.

Peace in the Forest

One day, the flamingo came to Son of the Forest, her face red with anger. The grass had told her of the snake's cruelty to the hunter. She told the hunter's son.

The snake was summoned and then commanded to tell its story.

"Yesssss, I did my part to send him away," the snake hissed. "He was a human! Humans are evil. He would have taken over the forest!"

Son of the Forest knew all that the gods had planned for his parents. The ancient turtle had told him. He was furious with the snake for interfering with the gods' plan.

He thundered, "Are you a god, that you dare to take on the work of the gods? This is not for you to do!"

Then Son of the Forest spoke to the

animals who had gathered there. "Today I become Papa Bois, Father of the Forest. I am responsible for what each of you does. From now on, there shall be no rivalry and fear among you animals. These feelings always bring pain. Snake, look how much pain your lie cost my mother! How hard it was for us to see her sorrow."

He continued, "I command you to love one another. That is how we drive out fear and keep peace in the forest. Yes, my father was a human. It is true that people are not like us. However, each human is different from the others. Therefore, each one must be judged separately."

For most animals, their ruler's command was easy to follow. The forest remained a happy, peaceful place.

Then, after many years, the ancient turtle returned. The forest buzzed with excitement. Animals wondered why the turtle had come. It seemed that whenever he appeared, something remarkable happened. Soon, something remarkable did happen.

An old man, hobbling along with a cane, came into the forest that same day. It was the hunter! The gods had led him back to the place where he had found peace.

Every animal lined up to greet him. The snake came but hung its head in shame.

"No more unhappiness," said the hunter. He looked at the snake and continued, "Let us be at peace with one another."

The parrot introduced the hunter to Papa Bois, the ruler of the forest, who was his son. The hunter asked, "Gionda? Where is she?"

"Patience! She is waiting for you," said Papa Bois. "First, come look in the pool."

There the hunter saw his reflection and smiled. He was a young man once more! He understood that the gods had given him a portion of their immortality.

Papa Bois explained that Gionda, too, would look as she had when she and the hunter were married. The hunter understood then that he and Gionda would live forever.

Papa Bois told the hunter to follow him to the sea, where the ancient turtle awaited him. At the turtle's direction, the hunter crawled onto the turtle's back. They began the journey to where Gionda waited.

Papa Bois went to his mountaintop and looked out over the forest to the ocean. He imagined his mother's joy at seeing her mate again. He laughed a laugh that could be heard all the way to Venezuela.

1. Who were the parents of Son of the Forest?
2. Why did the gods cause the hunter to leave the forest?
3. Why did Gionda have to teach her son all she knew so quickly?

The Island of Peace

> *The religion of Voodoo came to the Caribbean islands with the slaves from Africa. The most important and powerful Voodoo god is Damballah Ouedo. He is the father of all that is good.*
>
> *Slavery and fighting over the rich island plantations caused bloodshed and misery for the Caribbean people for centuries. In this story, the Haitian people ask Damballah Ouedo for the secret to peace.*

On the coast of Haiti is the city of Port-au-Prince. Some forty miles out to sea from this city lies the island of La Gonave. By the bright light of the afternoon sun, the people of Port-au-Prince can look out across the ocean and see the island.

Its mountains rise blue in the distance. The island's shape looks to the watchers like a giant whale with a woman sleeping peacefully on its back.

In fact, La Gonave is a peaceful place. Those who visit there feel a calm and quiet they have never known before. People call La

Gonave the Mother of Peace. Here is her story.

The Haitians longed for peace, yet they seemed never to have it. Years ago, the Europeans had brought slavery to Haiti. The slaves were forced to work on the rich sugar plantations. Fierce wars were waged for control of the plantations. Battles raged and rivers ran with blood. Almost all the people lived in poverty and misery.

The Haitian people prayed to Damballah Ouedo.

"Damballah Ouedo, you are master of the sky," they chanted. "Hear our cry! We have known whips and chains and fighting. Our blood and the blood of our ancestors has stained the sugarcane fields. Please let us know peace."

The great god was traveling through the sky. He heard the people's prayers and was moved. He spoke to one of his wives, Cilla.

"Cilla," he said, "you will take a message to my beloved people. You will take the secret of peace."

With that he gave Cilla the secret for peace. Then he commanded the Master of Waters to prepare a boat for her.

"Be sure it carries her safely all the way

to Port-au-Prince," Damballah told him.

"It shall be done," the Master of Waters replied. Then he summoned a great whale. He instructed it to carry Cilla safely and quickly.

The Master of Waters said to Cilla, "This whale will be your boat."

"Mind that you give her a ride of great comfort, too," he added to the whale.

The whale agreed and set out with Cilla on its back. The whale moved through the water with great speed yet very carefully. The gentle movement through the water caused Cilla to become sleepy. She fell fast asleep.

When they arrived at Port-au-Prince, Cilla slept on. The whale knew it dare not awake Damballah's sleeping wife. Cilla did not know she had reached Haiti. What could the whale do? The message of peace must be delivered, but how?

There was nothing to do but wait. The whale floated patiently in the harbor near Port-au-Prince. Days passed. Days turned into weeks and weeks into years, and still Cilla slept on. The patient whale and Cilla were still for so long that they became the island of La Gonave.

Cilla and the whale

Today, Cilla is still sleeping there, with the secret for peace in her hand. One day she will wake up and give it to the people of Haiti!

So La Gonave beckons, as it has for centuries. No Europeans went to settle there. Runaway slaves found safety on La Gonave, and there they found peace. For even in sleep, Cilla gives some of her secret of peace. She breathes peace into the air.

1. *Why did the Haitians long for peace?*
2. *What did Damballah Ouedo do when the Haitian people prayed for peace?*
3. *Why hasn't Cilla given the Haitians the secret of peace?*

The Pointing Tree

> *The city of Ponce is so beautiful that it is called the Pearl of the South. One of its great treasures is a huge ceiba tree, also called a silk-cotton tree. It is near the river beside the city of Ponce. It is so majestic and large that people say it is home for a god.*
>
> *For centuries, people have walked in the shade of this ceiba to enjoy the cool river breeze. For centuries people have told this story while sitting beneath its spreading branches.*

Long ago, Spaniards came to the island. Even then, the ceiba tree was old and mighty. The only people living there then were the peaceful Taino Indians.

The Spaniards brought with them iron swords. They had booming guns and high-stepping horses. The Indians soon learned to fear these strangers, with good reason.

The Spaniards meant to take the Indians' land, and they meant for the Indians to become slaves. When the natives objected, the Spaniards tried to force them. The Indians fought back, but they did not have any weapons to compare with swords and guns. Usually, they lost the battle.

One day, such a battle was raging. Spanish soldiers attacked a band of Indians, who fought them bitterly. The Taino were being beaten back. Since they did not want to be killed or taken as slaves, they fled across the river. They passed beneath the ceiba tree and hid themselves in the thick, tangled bushes near it.

The Spanish soldiers came charging across the river and stopped under the ceiba tree. Their horses snorted and stamped. The soldiers looked this way and that, wondering where the Indians had gone. The silent Indians watched them from their hiding place.

The soldiers stood there trying to decide which way to go. Suddenly, the forest became as still as a stone. Not one bird chirped. No insects buzzed from blossom to blossom. No lizards roamed the trunks of trees. Not a breath of air stirred. The forest might have been painted on canvas, it was so still. Time seemed to hold its breath.

Then, all at once, a great wind began to blow overhead. The branches of the ceiba rustled in an unusual way. The Spanish soldiers looked up and saw an amazing sight.

Every branch of that ceiba tree slowly swung in one direction. The branches formed themselves into a shape like a giant arm, pointing off into the distance.

"What's this?" the soldiers cried. "The tree is pointing!"

"It must be an omen!"

"Perhaps some spirit is pointing the way! That must be the direction the Indians have gone."

The soldiers believed the tree was guiding them. They rode off in the direction it pointed. It led them along a narrow trail that wound deep into the woods. It led them away from the bushes where the Indians hid.

The soldiers found thorny branches and tangled vines, but they could find no trace of Indians. They searched until they were exhausted. At last the soldiers admitted defeat. The commander ordered all of them to turn back.

When they reached the ceiba tree again, they paused and looked up. Its branches were spread out as usual, rustling gently in a cool breeze. Insects buzzed and sang, and birds chirped. The tree now seemed like a huge, green shelter, giving shade to all.

The ceiba tree pointing the way

The soldiers were perplexed. How, they wondered, could they have misread the sign of the tree? They gave up and went back across the river, never knowing the Indians were watching them.

The Indians knew, though, that a spirit lived in the ceiba tree. This spirit had saved them. It had pointed the Spaniards in the wrong direction.

The Indians told their children and grandchildren this story. Long after the fighting ended, the story was handed on to Indians and settlers alike. Even today, children know of the good and generous spirit of the ceiba tree.

1. *Where did the Indians hide from the Spaniards?*
2. *What did the Spaniards think the tree was showing them?*
3. *What did the Indians think the tree was trying to do?*

The Fireball Woman

In Trinidad, people tell stories about a terrifying being called a soucouyant. *In this story, a young man finds a way to rid the village of a soucouyant.*

A long time ago, an old woman lived in a village. Rather, her house was out beyond the edge of the village. It was a lonely place, and that was fine with her. She didn't want any prying eyes or noisy mouths around her. She wanted to be alone, because she didn't want anyone to know her secret.

Her secret was this: She was not really an old woman at all. She was a soucouyant!

By day she disguised herself as an old woman who slept most of the time.

As the sun went down, though, strange things began to happen. The birds that sang in her trees by day turned into bats in the evening. When it was dark, the soucouyant woke up. She began peeling off her skin. She peeled the skin off her arms. She peeled it off her legs. When she had peeled it all off, she packed her skin into a cool clay pot. Then she hid the pot in a secret place.

The soucouyant peeling off her skin

She hid it so carefully because she had to wear it by day. A soucouyant cannot let the daylight shine directly on her true form.

With her skin peeled off, the soucouyant appeared as her true self—a ball of fire! The fiery soucouyant began to rise up. She didn't want to set her house on fire, so she had to be careful. Slowly, slowly, she went through the roof. Dogs began barking and yowling. She let out a terrible shriek and sailed away into the night.

These noises terrified the villagers. They knew the soucouyant was flying. It wasn't safe to be out!

All the villagers rushed to finish their work outside before the sun set. Shoppers and traders at market made sure they started home well before dark.

They knew a lone person walking at night could meet a horrible fate. The soucouyant was searching all night for just such a person. If she found one, she would fly down on the person. She would burn the person and suck out all the blood.

All the people stayed within the four walls of their houses from nightfall to dawn. No one visited friends in the evening. There could be no great feasts or dances at night. It made life very boring and sometimes inconvenient. Only in this way, however, did people feel safe from the soucouyant.

One day, a young man moved into the village. He heard a shriek at nightfall and saw the terror of the villagers. He asked, "What is it that causes such fear?"

"The soucouyant! The soucouyant!" the villagers told him. The young man wanted to know all about her.

The villagers told the young man about the woman. They told him how she disguised herself as an old woman and slept all day. They told him about how she changed into a ball of fire at night. With their teeth chattering, they told of how she looked for human victims until almost dawn.

"She must put on her skin before day breaks," they explained. "The fire of the sun puts out the fire of the soucouyant."

As the young man listened, a plan began to take shape in his head. He said to himself, "I know how to get rid of this soucouyant!"

That evening, before the sun began to sink, he set out for the old woman's house. Bouncing in his pocket was a small bag of salt. He hid himself in the bushes next to the house and waited.

The sun set. The birds became bats. The young man watched as the soucouyant stripped off her skin. He saw her put her bundle of skin into the clay pot. He observed as she slid the pot into its hiding place.

Then he saw her rise up through the roof and heard her shriek as she flew off. This was the moment he had been waiting for.

The young man ran swiftly into the house and climbed up to the highest shelf. He found the pot of skin. He took the bag of salt out of his pocket. Then he sprinkled the salt all over the soucouyant's skin. He put the pot back in its hiding place. As soon as he had done that, he ran home fast, before the soucouyant could spot him from the sky.

Dawn was peeping over the horizon when the soucouyant flew back to her house. She reached for the jug and took out her skin. Just in time, she thought, for dawn was nearly there.

Because of the salt, the skin burned her badly. It slipped off and slunk away from her.

The soucouyant wailed and grabbed her skin again. She could feel that the sun was coming up, for her ball of fire flickered. Every time she slid the skin on, though, it slid right off.

"Don't you know me, Old Skin?" she wailed.

Then she realized someone must have put salt on it. It was too late, though. The sun's ball of fire had risen in the sky. The soucouyant's ball of fire grew smaller and smaller, then went out.

That night, the villagers had a party in the streets. The whole village rang with laughter and song and dancing. Not one person was hiding behind closed doors!

1. *Why did the old woman live in a lonely spot?*
2. *Why did villagers rush to get home before dark?*
3. *How did the young man destroy the soucouyant?*

Greedy Mariana

In Haiti, good manners are important, and a visitor should always be treated well. This story from Haiti tells what happens when an ill-mannered woman is visited by a zombie.

Mariana lived high up on a lonesome road, miles from the nearest village. She lived all alone, and it's little wonder that she did. She was a woman with a hot temper and a wicked mouth. She needed no excuse to give visitors a tongue-lashing. It was also her nature to take and take.

Sometimes travelers would find evening coming on as they walked on the high road. Only Mariana's hut would be in sight. The travelers would go to the door. They would say, "Could you just spare a crumb and a corner to sleep in?"

A sneer was the only greeting Mariana would give. The weary travelers were lucky to get a crumb. Perhaps Mariana would give out one bean and a few grains of rice. The corner of her hut was all she offered for a bed. A pillow and a blanket were too much to hope for.

At dawn the next morning, Mariana would awaken her guests—but not for breakfast. After she had used her big strong arms to take all their valuables, she would drive them away. She said, "Good riddance! Don't come back!"

One stormy night, Mariana was cooking sugarcane syrup to make candy. As she stirred the black pot over the fire, a knock sounded at the door.

The stranger politely called out the traditional greeting, "Honor."

"Respect," Mariana answered with a snarl, as she opened the door.

A man stood in the doorway, looking uncertain. "Please," he asked, "may I find shelter with you until the storm ends?"

Mariana nodded, craning her neck to see if the man had anything of value with him.

The man walked in, carrying a heavy bag. When he dropped it on the floor, it clinked loudly. Mariana's ears perked up. That was the clink of silver!

With a polite bow, the man backed into the storm again. He returned with another bag, just as full. It clinked the same way. He continued back and forth until there were four bags on the floor. Ah, that clinking sound was music to Mariana!

The syrup boiled away on the fire. Mariana began to shell peanuts to put in the candy. As she worked, she daydreamed about the silver. Mariana was brought out of her daydream when the man got up from where he was sitting.

The storm had ended. The traveler prepared to load his mules and continue his journey. He thanked Mariana with great courtesy.

"Hold it, sir," she said. "Where are your manners? I've given you shelter, and you think you'll leave without paying me? Shame on you!"

"A thousand pardons," the man said in a low voice. "Of course, I meant to pay you for your kind hospitality. Please choose any one of the four bags."

"*One?*" she cried. "Only one? My price is no less than *four!* Yes, that is what I charge for one hour's shelter. You are lucky that I don't charge you five or six bags!"

While she was ranting and raving, the stranger calmly tied three bags of silver on the mules. He started off, cracking his whip.

"Thief!" Mariana cried after him. "I want my money!" He just went on, as if he heard nothing. Mariana ran after him, screaming and yelling insults. The man paid no attention to her. He looked down as if he were lost in thought. The woman ranted and raved until she gasped for breath.

Still the man continued silently on his way. In the bags, the silver clinked a tune.

Mariana kept running after him. For hours they traveled along in the darkness. Not another soul was around.

Mariana warned, "Thief, I will take you to court. We'll see what the judges have to say. My syrup is burnt black by now. You'll have to pay me for that as well as the shelter!"

Then the man sang:
Greedy Mariana,
You'd better turn back now,
Or you'll be sorry!

Mariana was not only greedy and hot tempered, she was stubborn as well. How could she turn back, when three beautiful bags of silver were singing in their bags?

Dawn began to peep over a hill. A village was just around the bend. From somewhere, a rooster began to crow. When he reached the village cemetery, the traveler stopped.

Mariana was still howling, "My money! Give me my money!"

Mariana seeing the zombie

Suddenly, the mules disappeared. At that moment, the man turned and looked square into Mariana's face. What she saw was a skull with empty eye sockets and grinning teeth facing her. Bones clinked in the wind. They made the same tune that the silver in the bags had made.

Only then did Mariana realize that the traveler was no ordinary man. He was a zombie! He had come to get revenge for all the visitors she had mistreated and robbed. She had not heeded his warning. The zombie had made her look into his deathly face.

The shock was too much. Mariana fell down, dead. The zombie whisked away into the cemetery and vanished among the tombstones.

1. *How did Mariana treat visitors?*
2. *Why did Mariana run after the stranger?*
3. *Why did Mariana never get to collect the silver?*

The Magic Orange Tree

> *In the rural parts of Haiti, when a child is born, a seed from a fruit tree is planted. The tree that grows from the seed belongs to the child. Later the child sells the fruit that it bears. The tree is said to be the child's protector, or guardian. The girl in this story gets much needed help from her orange tree.*

Once upon a time, a girl was born to a man and woman who had very much wanted a child. It should have been a time of great happiness. It was not, however, for the mother died when the girl was still a baby.

The father and his daughter lived together quietly for some time. Then he decided to remarry. The man's second wife was evil and cruel, not at all like his first wife. She was so mean that some days she gave her stepdaughter nothing at all to eat.

The girl had always been quiet. Now she grew even more silent and pale. She was always hungry.

One day, like any other, the girl came home from school. Her stomach growled with hunger as it often did. Inside the house she found three oranges in the middle of the table. They were fragrant and ripe. The girl looked around the house but discovered no one there.

She peeled the first orange and ate it. It was delicious. Then she peeled the second orange and ate that, too. Now her stomach didn't pinch so much. She peeled and ate the last orange. It was just as sweet and good as the first two. Her stomach felt pleasantly full. She smiled happily.

Then she heard her stepmother coming home. She immediately thought that those must have been her stepmother's oranges! She quickly hid.

"Who stole my oranges from the table?" the stepmother asked. "Whoever did this wicked deed had better start praying! When I'm through with her, she won't even be able to pray!"

Fear gripped the girl, who trembled in her hiding place behind a chair. Surely her stepmother would kill her if she found her. So she ran through the door, up the road, and into the woods. She never stopped until she reached her real mother's grave.

There, completely exhausted, she fell in a heap. The moon rose and the owl awoke. Still the girl lay on her mother's grave, crying and praying. She prayed to her dead mother's spirit for help. At last she slept.

The morning rays of sun touched her face to wake her. She stretched and rose up on her knees. As she did, something fell from her apron to the ground. It was a single orange seed.

However, it was not just an ordinary orange seed. The moment it touched the earth, a sprout leafed out from it. Although the girl was astonished, she felt hopeful. She sang to the sprout:

>Orange tree, orange tree,
>Grow for me.
>Stepmother is not my mother,
>Oh, orange tree!

As she sang, the tree grew magically. Soon it was just her size.

She sang to it again, the same way. Again it grew. Branches grew from the tree, curving down and twisting up. They gave the tree fullness and they gave her heart hope. She sang again:

>Orange tree, orange tree,
>Flower for me.
>Stepmother is not my mother,
>Oh, orange tree!

Then lovely white flowers bloomed everywhere on the tree. As they withered, buds of fruit appeared to replace the blossoms. Now the girl sang:

> Orange tree, orange tree,
> Ripen for me.
> Stepmother is not my mother,
> Oh, orange tree!

Every bud ripened into a glowing orange. How her heart glowed then! The girl began to dance around and around the magic orange tree, singing her song.

Then she saw that the tree was growing larger and larger. It grew until the branches reached into the sky. She would never be able to reach the fruit now. Then she thought of another verse for her song.

> Orange tree, orange tree,
> Lower for me.
> Stepmother is not my mother,
> Oh, orange tree!

When the tree was a perfect height, she stopped singing and picked the fruit. Soon she was walking home with her arms loaded with beautiful oranges.

When she got home, her stepmother was there. As soon as the stepmother saw all those golden oranges, she grabbed them

The girl and the orange tree

away from the girl. The wicked woman ate every one.

Perhaps the sweet oranges improved her temper, for she spoke gently to the girl. "Tell me, my dearest, most clever girl, where did you find these wonderful oranges?"

The girl glanced up and then down, but she said nothing. She could see what would become of her oranges if she told!

The stepmother's temper had not really improved at all. She grabbed the girl's arm and twisted it cruelly.

"Tell me!" she barked. "Tell me where that tree is, or you will be sorry!"

The frightened girl led her stepmother through the woods. All the while, she was thinking. When they reached the tree, she was ready. She sang to the tree, asking it to grow again.

The orange tree grew so tall that the stepmother could not get any fruit. Again, the woman made her voice sound sweet and gentle.

"Oh, please, dear child," she begged, "I will give you many nice things to eat. You will always have as much as you wish. Make the tree smaller again. I promise I shall let you pick the oranges."

The girl thought to herself, and then she sang, very quietly. She asked the tree to lower, and it did.

As soon as its branches were her height, the stepmother leapt into the tree. Quick as a monkey, the woman climbed from branch to branch, gobbling oranges. She didn't take one from here and one from there. She seized every orange and stuffed it whole into her mouth.

"What will happen to me," thought the girl, "if I let her eat all the oranges?" Quickly, she sang to the tree and told it to grow. She kept singing, and it kept growing.

The stepmother ate so greedily, she didn't notice herself rising in the sky. When she looked down at last, it was too late. She could never jump so far and live.

"Help! Help me!" she cried. "H-e-l-p. . . ."

When the stepmother was just a dot against the sky, the girl cried, "BREAK, ORANGE TREE! BREAK!"

The tree shattered into countless pieces. The stepmother fell and was killed instantly.

The girl began to search among the branches. At last she found what she was looking for. With a smile, she picked up a single little orange seed. With the greatest care, she planted it on her mother's grave. She sang:

> Orange tree, orange tree,
> grow for me . . .

When the tree was just her size, she stopped. This time she took her fruit to market. Everyone wanted to buy such sweet, golden oranges!

Now she sells her oranges every Saturday at market.

1. *Why did the girl run away?*
2. *What happened to the orange seed that fell from the girl's apron?*
3. *What did the stepmother promise the girl in return for making the tree smaller?*

The Wedding Guests

This folktale is from Puerto Rico. In it, a young woman gets some help from fairies to make a happy marriage.

Once upon a time there lived a poor old sickly widow who was afraid of dying. She was not afraid for herself but for her daughter. The woman could not bear the thought of leaving the girl alone in the world. For this reason, she prayed each day for her daughter to find a good husband. She wished for someone kind and caring, so that her daughter would be happy.

The young woman was herself kind and good and hardworking. She was also pretty but so modest and quiet that most young men never noticed her. It was the girls who laughed and flirted who caught the eyes of those young men.

There was in that town, however, a rich fellow who was wise. He knew what he wanted in a wife. He wanted someone who was pleasant to look at but who was also goodhearted. He wanted someone who knew the value of hard work.

This man did notice the widow's daughter. The man admired the daughter and said so to the widow, who was happy to encourage him. She pointed out the beauty of her daughter's skin, her shining hair, and her tender ways. She would have been glad to point out more virtues, but the man interrupted.

"Yes, yes," he said, "I can see all that. However, I deal in cotton and silk. My wife must know all about the handling of fabric and thread. She must be able to spin, sew, and embroider expertly."

"Begging your pardon, sir," the widow said, "but my daughter is perfection with cotton and silk. She can do anything! Why, the thread she spins is like spider's silk. Her stitches are so small and even, they are like the footprints of tiny marching ants. She can embroider a butterfly that looks so real you would try to catch it in a net!"

The man was impressed. "Very well," he replied. "Since she is that talented, let the wedding be arranged!"

The widow watched him leave and went, full of joy, to tell her daughter what had been said. Her heart was so light, it might have been her own wedding she was announcing!

The daughter was not happy, however. In fact, she was miserable. She did want to marry the young man, but she was troubled by her mother's fine speech.

"Mama, how could you lie?" she protested. "You know I cannot sew a fine seam. I know even less about spinning and embroidery. The man will be furious with me!"

"Silly girl," her mother replied. "Every word I said was for your own good. Every problem has a solution. You have only to think of a solution for this problem."

These words didn't make the young woman feel a bit better. That night she lay awake, tossing, turning, and weeping. Her mother had told such terrible lies! What would become of her when her young man found he had been deceived?

Finally, she decided what she must do. She must go to him and tell him the truth about herself. It would take all her courage, but she was determined. The very next morning, that is just what she would do.

No sooner had the young woman decided this than she heard a light rustling in her room. What now! As if she hadn't enough trouble, there were three strangers standing before her! She wept more than ever.

"Do not weep," they said to her. "We mean you no harm. We are good spirits, fairies, and we can help you—if you will obey one condition."

The spirits told the young woman she must be sure that they were invited to the wedding. She agreed happily.

"You shall be welcomed as my dearest relatives," she said.

With that, the three fairies disappeared. The young woman was so relieved, she went right to sleep.

The next morning, she told her mother that she would be happy to marry the young man. Her mother was very pleased. She went right away to find the young man and tell him that the marriage would be arranged.

The days passed quickly, and the wedding plans were made. The bride-to-be made sure that three special guests would attend the feast.

"They are my favorite cousins," she explained to her husband-to-be, "and they simply must be included!" So the wedding list included the three spirits.

Finally, the great day arrived. A spectacular wedding took place. Everyone remarked about the bride's beauty. The groom smiled happily and made everyone feel welcome.

In the evening, everyone gathered in the banquet hall for the wedding feast. However, three chairs remained empty. Since they were placed near the bride, people were curious.

"Who is to sit here?" the new husband asked his bride.

Just then a knock sounded at the door. All eyes turned to look as it opened for the three tardy guests. The latecomers were old hags! The poor things were bent and misshapen in strange ways.

They took their seats. The room buzzed with clacking tongues. Some guests felt horror and some felt sympathy.

Mostly, it seems, everyone felt hungry. As soon as dinner was announced, they ate with hearty appetites. Every dish was pronounced most wonderful. The mood was light. The old hags seemed forgotten.

The husband had not forgotten the special guests. He was curious! After dinner, he approached his wife's cousins. After all, they were his cousins now, too, and he meant to get to know them.

Since he believed in plain speaking, the

groom spoke right out. "Cousin," he said to the first hag, "what has made you so hunched over? How did you lose one eye?"

"Ah, dear boy," she croaked, "all my life I embroidered. I bent over the stitches from dawn to dusk. That is what hunched my back and dimmed my eye!"

The husband stepped back in alarm. He whispered to his wife, "You must not ever embroider! Certainly it is worth a small cost to have this done by someone else. I don't want you to wind up like your poor cousin!"

He then approached the second hag. "Tell me, why do you have one long arm and one short one?"

"Ah," she sighed, "I spent my life spinning thread. Reaching and pulling, that's what made my arms unequal!"

The bridegroom reached for his wife's hand. "You shall never spin, my love!" he cried. "You must not ever use your spinning wheel."

Last, he asked the third hag, "What caused your eyes to pop out from your head like that?" Indeed, they looked like grapes that had slipped out of their skins.

"Your eyes would look the same," she said, "if you spent your life poring over tiny stitches."

The husband then said to his wife, "Your eyes shall never be like this. I do not want you ever to sew again! We will get rid of your sewing things."

The groom was as good as his word. The very next day, he heaped together all his wife's sewing things and made a great bonfire of them.

So the young woman never fretted about the lies her mother had told. She knew her husband truly cared for her. Her comfort, health, and beauty meant more to him than the work she could do. They lived together happily for many, many years.

1. Why was the young woman unhappy with her mother?
2. Why didn't the girl tell the young man the truth?
3. Why did the man forbid his wife to spin, sew, and embroider?

Bringing Back the Dead

> *Papa God appears in many Haitian stories. He is a likable spirit who takes a human form. Although he made the world, he doesn't usually interfere in the way it runs.*
>
> *In this story from Haiti, Papa God considers the wisdom of Dog's request to bring the dead back to life.*

Cat and Dog warmed themselves in front of the fire. All evening they talked about this problem and that problem. As usual, before long, Dog got around to his own problems.

"I can never get enough to eat," he complained. "If only there were more food!"

He thought a moment, then added, "More people! That's what we need on the earth."

"What are you saying?" asked Cat. "There are too many people as it is. There isn't enough food to go around. If there were more people, things would be even worse!"

Dog warmed his belly at the fire and thought. He said, "People give bones to dogs. If there were more people, there would be more bones for me."

He smiled, just thinking about all those bones. Suddenly, he jumped up. "That's it! I know how to get more food. I'll ask Papa God to bring the dead back to life. Then there will be people everywhere!"

"There are already people everywhere!" Cat cried. "How can we possibly make room for more?"

Dog thought a moment. Then he said, "You know people mourn the dead all the time. They have ceremonies to keep the spirits of the dead happy. The living should be glad to have the dead back if they miss them so much. Let them make room!"

So Dog planned what he would say to Papa God the next day. Cat made a plan too, however.

Before the sun rose, Cat went to the butcher. He bought eight nice meaty bones and started out to Papa God's house. Every now and then, he'd drop a bone in the middle of the path.

Pretty soon Cat was knocking on Papa God's door. At first no one answered.

"Hello! Papa God!" called Cat.

Finally, Papa God answered the door. Cat bowed low and spoke respectfully. "Papa God, please hear me out. I thought you would want to know the talk that is going around. Dog plans to ask you to bring back the dead. Yet there is not enough space or food for the people now living. Think of how noisy it will be with more people!"

Cat knew that Papa God loved peace and quiet. From the looks of it, Papa God enjoyed sleeping late, too.

"Just think what it will be like," Cat continued. "More houses will have to be put somewhere. People are likely to build houses clear up here by you! Since the dead have had to be quiet so long, they'll probably be extra noisy."

Papa God gave Cat a cup of morning coffee. While Cat sipped, Papa God considered. He thought about how lovely it was to be able to sleep in the quiet morning. He imagined the hammering and shouting from the extra people.

"I must think some more about this," he told Cat. Cat bowed low again and then left for home.

Late in the day, Dog arrived at Papa God's house. He had eaten eight bones he'd found on the trail, and his stomach nearly dragged the ground. He waddled up to where Papa God sat on his porch. "Papa God," began Dog, "you made me without giving me a way to earn food. In your wisdom, you made people be kind to me and give me food. Please, I ask you, won't you bring back the dead? Then there will be more food."

"What?" Papa God exclaimed. "You want food? Someone is feeding you like a king and you ask for more? I can't believe it!"

Papa God sent Dog away then and there. Dog tried making a little bow. He began to think he knew who had left those bones along the trail. There was nothing he could do now. So, home he went.

Thus, the dead remain dead. They do not return to the earth. Also, since that time, Dog has never trusted Cat.

1. Why did Dog want to bring back the dead?
2. Why did Cat think it was a bad idea to bring back the dead?
3. Why did Papa God refuse Dog's request?

Turtle's Trip

This story from Haiti also has animals as its main characters. It is intended to teach a lesson as well as to entertain. In it, a moment's foolish pride costs Turtle his fondest dream.

Excitement was in the air! Today the birds of Haiti would fly to New York City. All the animals gathered to watch the birds leave. This was to be a grand trip, and the gathering had a carnival feeling.

Turtle was not happy, however. More than anything, he wanted to fly to New York with the birds. It was impossible, of course, for his hard shell couldn't do the work of wings.

Turtle sat beside the water and hung his head. Pigeon, who had a kind heart, took pity on him. She said, "Turtle, I'll help you fly to New York."

"How?" Turtle asked eagerly.

"I'll take you with me," Pigeon replied. "I'll hold one end of a stick in my mouth. You bite onto the other end."

Turtle hurried to find a strong stick. He clamped onto one end of it and rushed back to Pigeon. He was just in time, for the birds were about to take off for New York.

"There's just one thing," Pigeon warned Turtle. "You must not let go of the stick, no matter what. If you do, you'll fall into the water below. I cannot land on water, so don't let go!"

Turtle nodded, and Pigeon took the free end of the stick in her beak. Up she flew, with Turtle dangling on the stick behind her. They were a remarkable sight!

The animals who had gathered by the ocean were waving good-bye to the birds. When they saw Pigeon and Turtle, they gasped and pointed.

Noisy chatter flew into the air.

"What's this?"

"Oh, look! Turtle is going to New York!"

"Lucky Turtle!"

The chatter reached Turtle's ears. Now Turtle seldom got much attention. When he heard all the animals talking about him, he was proud and pleased! Turtle thought quickly about what he could do to show his appreciation. He knew only one word of English, so he thought he would impress the watchers with it. He called out cheerfully, "Bye-Bye!"

Turtle made the mistake of opening his

Pigeon and Turtle

mouth! When he spoke, he let go of the stick and fell into the sea. Pigeon flew on her way without him.

That is why, to this day, there are many pigeons in New York, but turtles remain in Haiti.

1. *Why was Turtle unhappy?*
2. *How did Pigeon solve the problem?*
3. *Why didn't Turtle go to New York?*

The Parrot Who Wouldn't Say "Cataño"

An old sailor and a parrot would be common sights in a Puerto Rican seaport like Cataño. The Caribbean islands have hummed with sea trade since the time of Columbus.

In this story, both a sailor and a wealthy bird collector try to teach a parrot. However, it is the parrot who winds up teaching them a lesson.

San Juan, the capital city of Puerto Rico, is a busy seaport. Just across the bay from San Juan lies the town of Cataño. Long ago, an old sailor retired from the sea and made his home in Cataño. His only companion was his parrot.

The sailor didn't have much money, but he prized the parrot more than gold. The beautiful bird would chatter all day long. Anything a person would say, the parrot would repeat. She was the talk of the town. Everyone said this was the smartest bird in the world!

There was just one word the parrot did not say, and that was *Cataño*. Each day, the

The sailor and his parrot

sailor could be heard trying to get the bird to say *Cataño*. It would have meant a lot to him, for it was the town of his birth, and he loved it.

"Come on, now, say *Cataño*," the sailor would coax.

The bird would fluff her feathers, blink her eyes, and say something else. Was it that she *couldn't* or that she *wouldn't* say *Cataño*? Perhaps she thought it wasn't a very special word. Perhaps she didn't understand, like the sailor did, how rare a happy home is. It's hard to say.

However, she did seem to have a twinkle in her eye when the sailor begged her. She did seem to enjoy all the extra attention from her master.

It made the sailor sad that his beloved bird would never say *Cataño*. He didn't give up, though. Those who passed by his balcony could hear what sounded like an argument any day of the week.

"Say *Cataño*," the sailor pleaded.

The bird replied happily with a flood of words. Not one of them was *Cataño*. The sailor began to get very discouraged.

One day a rich fellow from San Juan happened along the street where the sailor lived. He heard the parrot talking and stopped to listen. The more he listened, the more amazed he became.

"Such a marvelous bird!" he thought. Now it happened that this man owned many fancy birds. He always had his eyes open to add to his collection.

"This bird will be like the jewel in my crown," he decided. "I must buy her!"

He approached the sailor and asked, "What will you take for the bird?"

"Not silver or gold," the sailor replied. This surprised the rich man, for it was clear the sailor had little money. The rich man wasn't used to taking no for an answer.

"I must have this bird!" the rich man cried. "I promise she will live like a queen! Name any price!"

The sailor thought a minute. It pleased him to think of his parrot living amid splendor. On the other hand, he hated to give her up! Then he had an idea.

"I'll make you a deal," the old sailor said. "If you can make her say *Cataño,* you may have her. I will die a happy man. If you cannot, then you must return her to me."

The rich man couldn't believe his good luck. He was delighted.

"Wonderful! Of course, of course," he said. He thanked the old man again and again, and he left with the parrot.

That very afternoon the rich man sat in his large, sunny courtyard, smiling and stroking the parrot.

"Now, my pet," he said, "you must say as I say, *Ca-ta-ño.*" Every syllable fell from his mouth just as clear as a bell.

The bird stared at him with her bright yellow eyes. She seemed to be thinking it over. She said nothing.

The smile left his face. "Come now, say *Ca-ta-ño.*"

The parrot tilted her head and cracked her beak but again said nothing.

"Listen here!" cried the rich man. "I know you can say *Cataño*. You can say anything!"

The parrot raised her wings and flapped them once, as if to say, "Humph!" Then she sauntered off across the courtyard.

This man had stacks of money, but his patience wouldn't fill a little bag. He flew into a rage hotter than a red chili pepper. He gritted his teeth and shook his fist. Then he ran after the bird and snatched it up.

"Stupid bird! Say *Cataño* or I'll kill you!" he cried.

He shook the poor parrot until her beak rattled. She blinked at him and wiggled away. Then the man seized her quick as a lightning flash. The look in his eye was like that of a madman.

"Stupid bird! Say *Cataño,* or I'll kill you!" he screamed again.

The parrot was as silent as a stone wall.

In a rage, the man dashed to one of his chicken houses and threw the bird inside.

"Stupid, stupid bird! More stupid than a chicken! Tomorrow I shall kill you like an old stewing hen!"

Then the man slammed off into the house and went to bed. Later that night, he was awakened by strange noises. Something was causing an uproar among the chickens.

"My prize chickens!" he cried. He thought a thief must be after them. He ran to the first chicken house and flung open the door. His jaw dropped with amazement and horror.

Feed and water pans were knocked all about. The floor was littered with the bodies of chickens. Other chickens ran around in terror while feathers rained down from the rafters. The man looked up to find the source of the terrible noise. His eyes came to rest on a rafter.

There was the parrot, clutching a prize fowl in her sharp claws.

"Stupid bird!" the parrot screamed. "Say *Cataño* or I'll kill you!"

Many chickens had failed to say the word, and the parrot had killed them. The man ran like lightning to save at least a few of his beloved fowl.

In the morning, the rich man took the ferry across the bay. He did not look well. He had just one thought in his mind: Get the parrot back to Cataño!

The sailor looked up in surprise when he saw the rich man returning so soon with the parrot.

He shook his head sadly. "Then you, too, have failed?" he asked softly. "She would not say *Cataño*?"

"She said *Cataño*, all right!" the flustered man cried. "You can have her back, though. I want no part of her!"

"What? How can this be?" the puzzled sailor asked. "You have won the bargain."

"She made a fool of me! She said *Cataño* all the while she was killing my prize chickens!"

A moment later, the happy sailor held his parrot. He smiled as he watched the rich man scurrying back to the ferry.

"Truly, you are no fool," he said as he stroked his parrot. Then he whispered, "Say *Cataño*."

"Cataño, Cataño," she replied, and clicked her beak smartly. The two of them were very happy together for the rest of their lives.

It takes a wise master to know a smart servant!

1. Why did the rich man want the parrot so much?
2. Why did the rich man throw the parrot into the chicken house?
3. Why did the rich man take the bird back to the sailor?

The Doctor Outwits Death

> *In this legend from the Dominican Republic, Death appears as a human character. A doctor must do some quick thinking to get the better of Death.*

Once there was a fellow who dreamed a big dream. He thought, "Once I find work for myself, I'm sure to become rich right away." He believed in his dream—but not in looking for work.

Death took a liking to this man. "He's my sort of fellow," he thought.

One day, Death approached the man and said, "See here, I like you. Because I like you so well, I'll look after you. Listen to me, and you'll be a great success."

Death continued, "I want you to become a doctor. Yes! Right away! I'll see to it that you cure any patient you touch. However, you must agree to my conditions."

Death saw that the fellow was listening carefully, so he explained the deal.

"When you enter the sick room, note where I am standing. If I stand at the foot of the bed, you may cure the patient at once. If

I stand at the head of the bed, then there is nothing to be done. You can go for a walk in the park, play a game of chess, or just sip lemonade. Leave the patient to me, though, for that one is mine."

The fellow agreed readily, for this sounded like his sort of job. He went to the city, where there were many patients who needed curing. Before long, he had cured dozens. Before much longer, he had cured hundreds. When he had cured thousands, his fame had spread. The rumor ran like the wind through the city: This doctor can work miracles!

Finally, the rumor reached the king's palace. The king was very happy to hear it, too, for his daughter was deathly ill. If anyone needed a miracle, it was the princess. Immediately the king sent for this doctor who could work miracles.

The doctor soon arrived at the palace. The king got right to the point. "The princess is very ill," he said. "Save her, and I shall give you half my kingdom. If my daughter agrees, you shall have her hand in marriage. Let her die, and I'll have your head chopped off!"

The doctor thought desperately, "Death, please be standing at the foot of the bed!"

What he said out loud was "Of course I'll cure her! I'll be happy to. Lead the way, Your Highness." In fact, Death had been very helpful so far. Death had stood at the foot of the bed so many times, the doctor forgot to fear him.

This time, however, Death loomed at the head of the bed. The doctor turned quite pale. He thought, "Ay, my soul! Are both the princess and I to die?"

This was a time for quick thinking. Fortunately, the doctor was a quick thinker. He grabbed the bedframe and yanked it around. In an instant, the foot of the bed was against the wall. Death now stood at the foot of the bed.

Death fumed while the doctor helped the princess to her feet. She was quite well. She looked lovingly at the doctor.

Death stormed out the door, vowing that he would have revenge.

The grateful king kept his word and arranged to share his riches with the doctor.

The king also arranged that the doctor and his daughter would be married. After some time, there was a wedding. The king was glad that the family would now include a good doctor.

The doctor was happy with his new life. He was now rich, and he didn't have to work. Now he was not even working with Death.

The doctor stayed inside the palace with the princess and the king as long as he could. He did not want to go out where he might meet up with Death. Nonetheless, one day the doctor decided to go out to buy a gift for the princess. He left the palace and walked into the village. Much later, when he was walking home, he felt something seize his sleeve. It was Death.

"Come along," Death ordered.

The doctor suddenly found himself high in the sky. Spread around him in the heavens were millions of little oil lamps. Some burned brightly; others burned very low. "Each of these lamps," Death said, "is for the life of a person on earth. It burns until the oil runs out. When the oil runs out, so does the life."

Then he pointed at one particular lamp.

"This one here has only five minutes more to burn," he continued. "This flame is yours, my clever fellow."

The flame spluttered above a little dab of oil. The doctor sighed.

"If it must be," he said, "it must be. I have a last request. Will you hear it?"

Death nodded.

"Add enough oil to my lamp to last just fifteen minutes. I wish to tell you a story. It's a fine one."

Death agreed and measured out exactly ten minutes' worth of oil. The doctor watched carefully. He took a deep breath and began his story. It was a good one, full of gentle words like "peaceful rest" and "lilting brook." Soon, Death's head began to nod. While Death slept, the doctor tiptoed to the oil supply and filled his lamp to overflowing.

In fact, the doctor filled it so full that he is living to this day.

1. What ability did Death give the doctor?
2. What would have happened if the doctor hadn't cured the princess?
3. How did the doctor outwit Death the first time?

Anansi's Riding Horse

Trickster tales are popular in Jamaica. Anansi, the spider-man, and Tiger are often at odds in Jamaican trickster tales. Both characters can speak and act like human beings. Though he is small and weak, the trickster Anansi never stops scheming to win what he wants. In this tale, Anansi and Tiger both want to marry the same girl.

A long time ago, Tiger walked on two legs. He was big, strong, and good-looking. All the other animals bowed to him respectfully when they saw him.

Selina was the most beautiful girl in the village. Tiger loved her, and he had his heart set on marrying her. His chances looked pretty good.

When she looked at Tiger, Selina saw his brilliant, shining eyes and his big bulging muscles. She heard his roaring, which was so loud it shook the trees. When Tiger entered a room, Selina noticed all eyes turned to admire him.

Anansi loved Selina, too. Anansi, however, was weak and ugly with a spider's sticklike limbs. His voice was like a thin reed, and no one could even see his eyes! When Selina looked at Anansi, she wanted to laugh.

Both Anansi and Tiger came to call on Selina each evening. One evening, Anansi hurried to arrive before Tiger.

"Selina," he said, "you give Tiger a lot of your attention. I wonder if you know who he really is."

Selina started to laugh. "Tiger is Tiger," she said. "Who else would he be?"

"I'm surprised no one has told you," Anansi said, shaking his head sadly.

"Told me what?"

"Why Tiger is just my father's old riding horse!"

Selina stopped smiling. She was not only very beautiful, she was also very proud. It wouldn't do for her to marry an old riding horse.

"I don't see how that is possible, Anansi!" she said. "Tiger is a big strong fellow."

"Why, it's true!" said Anansi. "I used to ride him when I was little. Just watch! I will do it again!"

He scurried away just as Tiger came in, smiling broadly. "Selina, girl of mine, I love you," he said. "What do you say we two get married?"

Selina didn't know what to do.

"Tiger, tell me true," she said, "Is what Anansi said true?"

"What's that?" Tiger asked.

"Are you his father's old riding horse, for that is what he claims! I can't marry any riding horse!"

Tiger's roar of rage shook the trees for miles around.

"He is a liar," roared Tiger, "and I will prove it! I will bring Anansi here to confess his lie. Gather the animals together. I want witnesses."

Then Tiger thundered off at top speed to Anansi's house. Animals scampered out of his way. Small trees and bushes were smashed. Deafening roars filled every nook and cranny.

In front of Anansi's little house, Tiger stopped. In his loudest, most scornful voice he called, "Anansi, you are a rotten liar! Come out here right now!"

The little house wobbled as though it would fall. Roaring, Tiger kicked down the door and went in.

Anansi was in bed with the covers pulled

up to his tiny eyes. He moaned and groaned terribly.

"Now I've got you! You're coming with me to tell Selina what a dirty rotten liar you are!" he cried. He grabbed Anansi by one foot and dragged him from the bed.

Anansi kept moaning and groaning. His eyes were glazed like a dying man's.

"No, no, I can't," he said weakly. "I'm so sick. I'm dying. Let me die in peace, Tiger."

"No!" Tiger roared. "You can't die until you tell Selina the truth!"

"I'm too weak, Tiger," he said in his thin little voice. "The walk will surely kill me." Tears came to his eyes. He was a pitiful sight.

"Then I'll carry you," said Tiger, "but you must come now! Come on! Come on!" he roared. "You have to tell Selina I'm not your father's old riding horse! Then, if you aren't dead already, I'm going to kill you!"

"Very well," whispered Anansi, "but you must stoop down so that I can ride on your back. Carry me gently, or I will surely fall off." His voice was getting weaker and weaker, and he was beginning to shiver.

Tiger thought perhaps Anansi was near death. He stopped his roaring and started worrying about getting Anansi out of there quickly. Then Tiger put his front feet on the ground so that Anansi would not fall off.

"My blanket," Anansi whispered. "Get my blanket."

"What do you need with a blanket?" Tiger asked.

"My body is sore," he replied. "I will never make it to Selina's house without padding under me."

Tiger grumbled, but he did spread the blanket on his back. Anansi climbed up on Tiger's back and sat there, holding his head and moaning.

When Tiger moved off, Anansi began to slip and slide. He nearly fell to the ground. He moaned, "Tiger, Tiger, stop! Let me fall down and die!"

"I won't let you die yet! Not until you tell the truth! After that, I'll kill you my own self. Now what's wrong?" Tiger's paws itched to run quickly, before Anansi could die.

"I'm too weak to hold on," whined Anansi. "I will fall off as soon as you start moving and I will be killed."

"Then let's get a rope and tie you on," the impatient Tiger suggested.

Tiger tied the rope around his own neck

and told Anansi to hold on to it. Then he moved off, not as quickly as he would have liked. Anansi sat on his back, holding on to the piece of rope and moaning gently.

Pretty soon, Anansi began whining again. "Stop! Stop! I'm dying. Oh, I'm dying!"

Tiger stopped in alarm. He couldn't think of anything but getting to Selina's house with a live Anansi.

"What's wrong now?" he asked.

"It's the wasps and flies," groaned Anansi. "They're killing me! Could you please hand me that stick to keep them off me?"

"Very well," Tiger said impatiently. He handed Anansi the stick and hurried on.

At long last, they reached the clearing where Selina lived. They saw her standing on her porch. With her were Rat, Monkey, Cow, Snake, and Goat.

"Now," thought Tiger gleefully, "he'll tell the truth. Then I'll kill him!"

Suddenly Anansi sat up straight as an arrow and dug his heels into Tiger's sides. He yanked the rope and whacked Tiger smartly with the stick.

"Get up! Get up, Tiger!" he cried in his loudest voice. "Didn't I tell you, Selina? Tiger is my father's old riding horse!"

Anansi riding Tiger

Selina's eyes bulged nearly out of her head. Tiger yelped with pain and bolted. He was so embarrassed he wanted to get out of there fast. He stayed down on all four legs so he could run faster. Ever since, Tiger has been going around on four legs.

Tiger shook Anansi off his back at last. Anansi scooted up a tree. He has lived in trees ever since, staying out of Tiger's reach.

1. *What did Anansi tell Selina about Tiger?*
2. *Why did Tiger agree to let Anansi ride on his back to Selina's?*
3. *Why did Anansi really want the blanket, rope, and stick?*

Bouki's Dance

In this story from Haiti, the cunning trickster Ti Malice wants to outwit a king who loves to dance. To do so, Malice uses his greedy friend Bouki. In Haiti, this story is told to a group, and listeners join in on the singing and dancing.

The King's Contest

Haiti once had a king who loved to dance. He would rather dance than eat or sleep! The king wasn't rich. If he had been, he would have paid hundreds of dancers to perform for him every night.

As it was, the king contented himself with sitting in his garden after dinner. There he dreamed up new dance steps every night. Since a dance needs music, he thought of songs every night, too.

One night, when he was sitting in the garden, he began singing a new song. He liked it so well, he stood up and made up a dance to go with it. As he sang, he swayed and whirled around. His feet danced the fancy steps neatly.

This is the song the king sang:

> Kokioko, oh, Samba,
> Now I dance like this,
> Now I dance like that,
> Samba dance, ah, Samba dance!

Samba means "master musician." Clearly, the king was proud of his song and dance. In fact, the more he swayed and whirled, the more impressed he became.

"There never has been such a wonderful dance!" he thought. "No one in the world could create one half as good."

He began to have an idea. He would have a contest. Anyone who could dance his kokioko dance would win a big prize.

The king's treasury had little money in it, but the king wasn't worried about giving a prize. No one could possibly know the dance, so no one would ever win. What is more, the king would have many evenings to watch all kinds of dancers. It would cost him nothing. He congratulated himself for his cleverness and went to bed.

The next morning, the king made an announcement. Anyone who could dance the kokioko would receive money, 5,000 gourdes, from the king's own hand. With 5,000 gourdes, a family wouldn't need to work hard anymore, and they would eat very well.

The next night, hundreds of people lined the road before the king's palace. They wore fancy dancing clothes. Many of them had made amulets to wear around their necks. They hoped these magic pouches would help them guess the steps in the king's dance.

That night, the king saw the most marvelous dancing he had ever seen. No one could dance quite the right steps in quite the right order, though. No one guessed how to dance the kokioko.

It was the same the next night and the night after that. Music and singing filled the air. Nimble feet flew, and graceful bodies swayed. The king watched in delight. After every dance, the king would shake his head. No, that was not it.

One time a dancer got the first steps right. Another time, a dancer did the first and second parts exactly right but got the rest wrong. No one danced the entire dance as it should be.

For months, the dancing entertained the king. He never got tired of it.

When everyone had left, the king would go to his garden. There he would practice his kokioko dance. It wouldn't do for him to forget it!

One day, Ti Malice, the king's gardener, forgot his hat. He returned for it that night. As he got ready to leave the garden, he heard singing.

> Kokioko, oh, Samba,
> Now I dance like this,
> Now I dance like that,
> Samba dance, ah, samba dance!

Malice tiptoed soundlessly toward the sound. His eyes drank in greedily what he saw there in the moonlight. It was the king dancing the kokioko!

When he was sure he had memorized the dance, Malice ran home to tell his wife.

The next morning, he ran to visit his friend, Bouki.

"Honor!" Malice said in the traditional way.

"Respect!" Bouki replied.

Malice put a kind expression on his face. "Bouki, old friend," Malice said, "after all these years, I'm finally able to do something for you. It's something wonderful!"

"Oh-oh," said Bouki. He did know that when Malice set out to help you, things never seemed to work out well. You ended up worse off than when you started.

"No thanks," Bouki said. "I've had enough of your tricks!"

"Oh, well," Malice said with a shrug, "if you really don't want to be rich . . ."

"Well, it won't hurt to hear you out, I suppose," Bouki said.

"Bouki, last night I saw an amazing thing," Malice said. "I watched the king in his garden dancing the kokioko! He didn't know I saw. I learned every step by heart, but I cannot dance it for him. I'm his servant. He'd think I was spying. You could dance it for him, however."

"How?" Bouki snorted. "I didn't see it."

Malice shook his head. "I will teach it to you, of course, unless you don't want the 5,000 gourdes."

Bouki considered. With 5,000 gourdes, he could feast on fat oxen and sheep every day. No one loved to eat as much as Bouki. His mouth watered.

"Very well," he said, "Show me the dance."

Malice sang and danced:

Kokioko, oh, Samba,
Now I dance like this . . .

Bouki tried to follow along, but he was so fat and clumsy that he lost his balance. He fell down.

Malice could see this wasn't going to be easy. "I'll come back every night," he said.

"Every night you will learn a little bit of the dance."

It did take some doing, but finally Bouki knew every step in the dance. Several months later, Bouki stood in line outside the palace. He waited for his turn to dance for the king.

The dance wasn't graceful, but Bouki did dance the kokioko correctly. The king sat there stunned. How had it happened? He would have to give Bouki the reward.

It was a sad king who emptied his treasury. It was a joyous Bouki who ran from the palace carrying a heavy bag full of 5,000 gourdes.

Malice's Trick

"Malice! I won! I won!" Bouki cried as he carried away the king's gourdes.

The two friends danced and joked their way into the forest. Under a huge tree, Malice suddenly stopped.

"Bouki," he said. "You're a fine dancer to be able to dance the kokioko."

"Oh, yes," smiled Bouki.

"Now I have another dance to teach you. A simple dance."

Malice swayed his behind back and forth.

Bouki dancing the kokioko

With his eyes closed, he sang:
>If you're simple as this,
>Put your bag down and dance.

"Why that's too easy!" Bouki scoffed. He began to copy Malice's movements.

"Good! Good!" Malice cried. Then he began to sing and dance faster. His whole body shook.

Bouki put down the bag, closed his eyes, and shook his whole body as he sang:
>If you're simple as this,
>Put your bag down and dance.

He never saw Malice's wife creep out from behind the tree. She grabbed the bag full of gourdes and ran!

When Bouki opened his eyes, he cried, "Where is my bag?"

Malice's eyes got big. "Oh-oh," he said, hiding a smile, "you didn't put it on the ground did you, Bouki?"

"Yes, of course I did!"

"Bouki, you didn't listen! I tried to warn you!" Malice said.

Then he danced and sang his way into the night:
>If you're simple as this,
>Put your bag down and dance!

Bouki swore he would never listen to

Malice again! Of course, he did, but that is another story!

1. Why did the king offer a large reward when he had so little money?
2. Why couldn't Malice dance the kokioko for the king?
3. How did Malice get the 5,000 gourdes?

The Servant

> Characters in legends can be pitted against spirits. In this story from Cuba, a clever man must outwit the devil himself.

Once there was a wandering sort of fellow named El Bizarrón. He was always restless, always looking for work.

One time El Bizarrón learned that the devil needed a servant. Without a second thought, he decided to apply for the job.

"Be very careful!" he was warned. "The devil is a bad one. His last two servants disappeared mysteriously. Everyone who goes to work for him disappears. Probably he kills them."

"He doesn't scare me," El Bizarrón said scornfully. "He'll hire me and he'll be lucky to get me."

With that, he strode off to the devil's front door and pounded on it.

The door opened, and there stood the devil himself.

"Do you have work to give a strong fellow?" El Bizarrón asked.

The devil looked him up and down. "My

work could keep six of you busy," he replied.

Then he asked the fellow in and showed him his room. "Sleep well," the devil said. "You'll need the rest! Tomorrow I will put you right to work."

In no time, El Bizarrón's snores were shaking the whole house.

"He's not afraid, anyway," the devil said, as he planned his new servant's first job.

The next morning, the devil ordered El Bizarrón to carry water from the river. Then El Bizarrón gave an order right back.

"Bring me a pick and a shovel!" he said.

The devil raised his eyebrows a little, but he did as this new servant said.

El Bizarrón marched down to the river and began digging a ditch at once. The Devil watched him work. It looked like the ditch would be a long one.

Soon, the devil became impatient. "I said I wanted water, not a ditch!" he told his servant. "What on earth are you doing?"

"Why should I carry water when I can cause water to flow to you? I am making a canal from the river to your house. Then there will be no need to fetch water," El Bizarrón said.

The devil stared hard at the ditch. The

man was a worker all right. However, the devil had an uneasy feeling.

"He's a worker, but he's a thinker, too," he thought. The devil hadn't much use for clever thinkers. He wandered back to his house without comment.

Another day the devil wanted wood. He ordered El Bizarrón, "Go and gather wood for my fireplace."

"Very well," his servant replied. "Fetch me a long rope then."

The devil decided he wouldn't ask why but just handed El Bizarrón the rope. El Bizarrón went whistling off to the mountain, with the rope thrown over his shoulder. Not too far behind him slunk the devil.

A good-sized forest grew on the mountain slopes. Once he arrived, El Bizarrón began stretching the rope from tree to tree. He walked all around the mountain, roping the whole forest! Pretty soon, the rope wrapped up the whole mountain, just like a necktie on a neck.

The Devil could stand it no longer! He burst out, "What are you doing?"

"Why, I'm only tying up the forest. That way I can bring it all to your house in one trip," El Bizarrón said.

"This is no ordinary human," thought the devil. Somehow, the thought didn't make him feel at ease. He sent his servant back home without the mountain of trees. There was no room in his yard for so much wood anyway.

Some days later, a throwing contest was announced. The contestants would see who could throw a metal bar the farthest along the beach.

"Now here's something useful my servant can do for me," the devil thought. "He is certainly strong enough. I'll just have him win a prize for me." This thought cheered the devil considerably.

Soon they set off for the beach. The devil walked in front. El Bizarrón swung along behind, with a metal bar on his shoulders.

The beach was a lively place. Contestants were practicing their throws and stretching their muscles. El Bizarrón did not bother to practice. He threw himself down on the sand and went right to sleep.

He kept sleeping while the hours passed and the metal bars flew. Finally, it was time for him to throw.

"Up! Up!" the devil cried.

El Bizarrón opened his eyes. In a loud voice he said, "See those boats far out to sea?

Have them moved out of the way, or else my shot will sink them!"

The boats were too far away, though. It was not possible to send a message to them. Therefore, El Bizarrón would not be allowed to throw.

The devil was disappointed. More and more, he felt uncomfortable to have such a strong servant. Then there was the matter of El Bizarrón's brains. Such an ox with fox's brains, the devil reasoned, could be quite dangerous. He made up his mind to be rid of his servant.

All the way home, the devil was very pleasant to El Bizarrón. Once at home, the devil stretched himself out to sleep on the iron bars of the barbecue grill.

"Why not sleep underneath the grill?" the devil said to El Bizarrón. "It's the most comfortable spot!"

El Bizarrón said he would, but he noted the devil had become bulkier than usual. He was very suspicious of this.

In fact, the devil had taken two giant boulders to bed with him. He intended to drop them and crush his servant as he slept.

So the master lay on the grill above and the servant lay on the ground beneath.

Secretly, however, El Bizarrón then scooted himself to the far corner. There he kept a wakeful eye.

Around midnight, El Bizarrón heard a terrible noise. Right away, he said, "Ay, the mosquitoes are bad tonight. I believe one has bitten me!"

The devil was amazed. He had dropped two boulders, and they felt like a mosquito bite to this fellow! The devil's step was a little unsteady as he climbed down to see the damage.

By this time, El Bizarrón had moved and was now sitting under the barbecue. There wasn't a mark on him, but all around him were bits of smashed rock.

El Bizarrón said innocently, "You know, it wasn't a mosquito at all. It was these rocks. How do you suppose they got here?"

The devil's chin began to tremble and his teeth began to clatter. He said fearfully, "Good man, I'll give you a mule and all the silver it can carry. In return, I only ask you to leave. Go far away! Go to the moon if you can! Go farther!"

El Bizarrón said, "Why not?"

Pretty soon he was on his way, leading a mule with several saddlebags that bulged with money. The devil breathed a sigh of relief.

Before long, however, the devil's wife scolded him, "How could you be so stupid! He's not so strong. He just fooled you." Each sneer struck his pride like a whip. Could he possibly have been wrong? He must get that fellow back!

The devil saddled a horse and galloped after El Bizarrón, his mule, and his silver.

El Bizarrón heard hooves and looked back. He saw the devil catching up fast! He hid the mule in the sugarcane beside the road. Then he lay in the dusty road, sticking his legs up at the sky.

When the devil found him like this, he was at first speechless. When he found his voice, he asked, "Whatever is the matter with you now?"

"Not a thing, not a thing," El Bizarrón replied. "That stubborn mule wouldn't budge. I gave him a kick that sent him sky high. He disappeared into the clouds."

The devil's teeth started clattering again. "So why are you moving your legs around in the wind?"

"Why, the mule will fall back to earth sooner or later. I certainly don't want to carry that heavy silver myself! I'm going to break that mule's fall so he won't be killed!"

That clattering in the devil's teeth spread through every bone in his body. He shook like a leaf in the wind! Then he hauled his horse around and spurred it all the way home.

"Where's the servant?" his wife asked.

"What do I want with him?" the devil replied. "He had kicked the mule to heaven. Well, he might do the same to me, and heaven is no fit place for a devil! I'm only happy that he's gone. May he never return!"

1. *How did people think the devil usually treated his servants?*
2. *Why didn't El Bizarrón throw the metal bar in the contest?*
3. *How did the devil try to kill El Bizarrón?*

Why Rabbit Has Long Ears

In this story from Cuba, Rabbit is discontent with the size the Creator has given him. He wishes to be bigger. However, his ability to outwit larger animals shows he is very smart, if not very large.

The Creator drew a deep breath. At last, creation was nearly finished. It had been quite a task! Then he noticed Rabbit standing before him. The little creature had come to discuss a problem.

"Creator, sir," Rabbit said.

"Yes, Rabbit?" the Creator asked.

"Ah, you are able to see me. That's a change! It doesn't happen often."

"What doesn't happen often?" the Creator asked, a little puzzled and very tired.

"It isn't often that anyone sees me," Rabbit explained. "The problem is, I'm so small. If only you could have been a little more generous when it came to my size! You did give me speed. I'm furry and soft, and I cannot complain there. You were most generous to make me so handsome."

The Creator couldn't help thinking that

Rabbit also had a great supply of vanity.

The little creature continued, "However, it does no good to be quick or soft or handsome if you cannot be seen. I don't mean to be greedy. I'd just like to be a little bigger."

He dreamed a little. He added, "Of course, it would be wonderful to be as big as Camel or even as big as Elephant. How much more impressive would be my great quickness, my good looks, and my style and grace."

"Ahem!" the Creator interrupted.

Rabbit quickly said, "I meant as big as Goat. Yes, Goat's size would content me very well." Then he let a tear drop and bowed his head a little.

The Creator sighed and rubbed his chin thoughtfully. This was a tricky problem. Creation was no easy matter. Each animal had been measured out to an exact size. He didn't like to think of making changes.

Suppose he were to take some size from Whale and give it to Rabbit. No, that would not do. Whale was happy being the biggest creature.

The Creator thought about borrowing a little size from Camel. Perhaps she wouldn't miss one hump. No, Camel was already a great one for sulking. If she lost anything, she might just refuse to carry burdens.

What about borrowing from Grasshopper? No, that was ridiculous. There would be nothing left of Grasshopper!

The Creator sighed more loudly. Then he had an idea. He said, "Rabbit, if you truly want more size, you must work for it. Here is your task. You must bring me first an eagle feather, then a snake egg, and then a lion tooth. If you can do this, then I will consider your request."

Now Rabbit had to think how he could get these things. Since his thoughts were as speedy as his legs, it didn't take long.

He found a gourd and made himself a whistle. Then off he went to the mountain, whistling loud and clear.

Pretty soon, Eagle heard and came flying down. Rabbit quickly hid the whistle.

"What's all the racket for?" Eagle asked, frowning at Rabbit.

"Oh, dear," Rabbit replied, "I hope I haven't bothered you. It's just that I have a whistling hair on my side. It whistles once a day, rain or shine. When it does, a crowd of animals comes to me. I can choose any one I want for dinner."

Eagle looked very interested now.

Rabbit continued, sadly, "Of course, this gift is a bother to me. I don't care to eat animals. Instead, they chase me! It's a shame and a waste. Well, maybe someday I'll grow to like meat for dinner."

Suddenly Rabbit got a gleam in his eye. "I have it!" he cried. "All the animals are afraid of you. If you will only give me one of your feathers to wear, they might give me some respect. In return, I will then give you my whistling hair. Perhaps it will be of some use to you."

Eagle was only too happy to make the exchange.

Cheerful Rabbit went thumping on over the mountain, with Eagle's feather tucked behind his ear. He began to whistle again. Pretty soon Snake came crawling from under a thorny bush.

Rabbit told his tale again. He looked sad as he ended it. "All sorts of little animals come running to me—mice, rats. I cannot eat them. Really, though, what I am hungry for is an egg."

Snake couldn't stop thinking about those tasty little animals. She wanted that magic whistling hair! They agreed to trade. "Help yourself," Snake hissed, showing Rabbit her nest of eggs. Rabbit hopped away with one of Snake's eggs tucked in his ear.

In a short while, he came to Lion's cave. The great beast was dozing in the sun until he heard Rabbit's whistle. He gathered his face into one big scowl.

"Roaring thunder!" Lion said. "Stop that awful noise!"

A fainthearted animal would have run away, but not Rabbit!

"Forgive me, King Lion," he begged. "It's not me, but this bothersome hair on my side. It insists on whistling up dinner for me. If only it whistled up nice green shoots and buds! Alas, it calls out animals to be eaten! Then the animals chase me. If only I could have one of your teeth, the animals would respect me. I would gladly trade."

Lion thought this was a fine idea. He had many teeth and would not miss one, but every day he was hungry for animals to eat. Quickly he pulled the tooth out and traded for the hair.

Rabbit made his way speedily back over the mountain. He presented the tooth, egg, and feather to the Creator. The Creator was amazed.

The Creator said, "Is it possible that one

so small does such great deeds? How can I make you one inch bigger? If I did, you would do such things that all the animals would pester me. They'd want more size, or more protection, or more something else."

He stopped talking and looked at the sad little Rabbit. "What can I do?" he continued. "You are mighty enough as you are."

However, the Creator could not stand to see Rabbit so disappointed. He reached for Rabbit's ears and began to pull on them. When they were the length of an ear of corn, he stopped pulling.

"Now go away, Rabbit. You have speed, softness, handsomeness, and now big ears. I will not make the rest of you bigger, for that would cause trouble. The world has enough problems as it is!"

With this, Rabbit had to be content. To this day, rabbits have big ears, though their bodies are still small.

1. *What three things did Rabbit have to get before the Creator would consider his request?*
2. *What did Eagle trade Rabbit for his feather?*
3. *Why didn't the Creator give Rabbit a bigger body?*

Pronunciation Guide

Every effort has been made to present native pronunciations of the unusual names in this book. Sometimes experts differed in their opinions, however, or no pronunciation could be found. Also, certain foreign-language sounds were felt to be unpronounceable by today's readers. In these cases, editorial license was exercised in selecting pronunciations.

Key

The letter or letters used to show pronunciation have the following sounds:

a	as in *map* and *glad*
ah	as in *pot* and *cart*
aw	as in *fall* and *lost*
ch	as in *chair* and *child*
e	as in *let* and *care*
ee	as in *feet* and *please*
ey	as in *play* and *face*
g	as in *gold* and *girl*
hy	as in *huge* and *humor*
i	as in *my* and *high*

ih	as in *sit* and *clear*
j	as in *jelly* and *gentle*
k	as in *skill* and *can*
ky	as in *cute*
l	as in *long* and *pull*
my	as in *mule*
ng	as in *sing* and *long*
ny	as in *canyon* and *onion*
o	as in *slow* and *go*
oo	as in *cool* and *move*
ow	as in *cow* and *round*
s	as in *soon* and *cent*
sh	as in *shoe* and *sugar*
th	as in *thin* and *myth*
u	as in *put* and *look*
uh	as in *run* and *up*
y	as in *you* and *yesterday*
z	as in *zoo* and *pairs*

Guide

Capital letters are used to represent stressed syllables. For example, the word *ugly* would be written here as "UHG lee."

Anansi: uh NAN see

Arawak: ah rah WAHK

Bouki: BOO KEE

Carib: KAR ihb
cassava: kuh SAH vuh
Cataño: kuh TAHN yo
ceiba: SEY buh
Cilla: SEE luh
Damballah Ouedo: dam BAHL ah WAY do
El Bizarrón: ehl bee sah RON
Gionda: jee AHN dah
Kabo Tano: KAH bo TAH no
kokioko: ko kee O ko
La Gonave: lah go NAHV
Papa Bois: PAH pah BOY
Ponce: PON se
Port-au-Prince: PORT o PRIHNS
sapodilla: SAHP uh DEE yuh
soucouyant: soo KEE ya
Taino: TI no
Ti Malice: TEE mah LEES